Telegraph 2000

LOUTH

The Twentieth Century

DAVID  H

Dilke Publishers
49 Linden Walk, Louth,
Lincs., LN11 9HT

First Published 1999

Copyright © David Cuppleditch

Cover photographs –
Front: Fish and Chip Tramp Supper –
   Louth, 8 November 1955
Back: Postcard of Louth (circa 1910)

British Library
Cataloguing in Publication Data
ISBN 0-9506244-4-6

Typesetting, origination and Printing
by F. W. Cupit (Printers) Ltd.,
The Ropewalk, 23 Louth Road,
Horncastle, Lincs., LN9 5ED

Below: One firm that has survived is Larder's. This bill dated 22nd December 1841 was addressed to William Scrope Esq. of Cockerington Hall.

Opposite: And this bill to Mr. Ackrill was from Robert Norfolk. Louth Navigation Society is trying desperately to re-open the waterways of the old Louth Canal, mostly with the help of volunteers. It was the Louth flood of 1920 that finally killed off the water traffic that once plied between Riverhead and the North Sea.

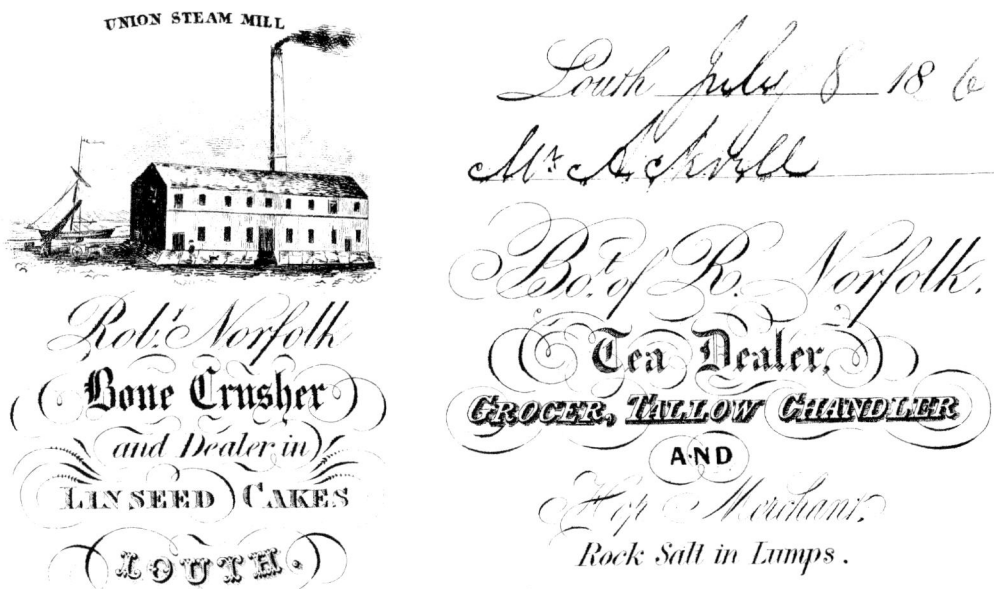

INTRODUCTION

This book celebrates Louth's millennium and will fascinate anyone remotely interested in Louth history. Much has happened in the last hundred years, both in terms of values and morals as well as architecture.

Modern-day Louth sprawls over a much larger area than it did 50 years ago! With fields and nurseries turned into modern housing estates. In the fifties and sixties Louth had a comfortableness that could compare with deja vue, in that you could leave a bar, go halfway around the world and return two or three years later to find the same people standing in more or less the same place where you'd left them. That was Louth's strength. Its inhabitants were always courteous and hospitable to strangers; and certain buildings, like the old Corn Exchange, looked as if they had just been transported off a film set. Inside the Corn Exchange the smell of wheat and barley was overwhelming. You could almost visualise the seed merchants dressed in gaiters and boots who traded there a century before. Sadly, it remained unused for many years with occasional furniture auctions until it was finally demolished and the Halifax Building Society offices were erected on the site.

In those days the Cattle Market flourished, with "beests" of every description and cattle trucks blocking Newmarket. There was a section for sheep at the top end just below the Snowden's house (also demolished). Heifers and bulls occupied the central area and the pig market had its own covered roof. Funnily enough, the pigs were probably the noisiest of all.

Farmers would frequent the town's hostelries after their day's trading and would wend their merry way home, occasionally inebriated.

Louth seemed to possess a much more colourful selection of characters then and people were not cloned to their computers; nor did they try to converse in computer-speak. One great character was Jack Blythe's son, William, who worked on the Cattle Market for years, helping auctioneers and sluicing down the pens after the market. (Jack Blythe was Louth's last Town Crier). William Blythe used to be allowed to miss school on Fridays in 1899, (then a lively nine year old boy) to meet the 7.30am cattle train and see that the stock was delivered to market. Another was the flamboyant "Theo" (Theodore) West, who accumulated fortune through various agricultural deals and expanded into horse racing. His usual attire was a broad-brimmed hat, tilted at a rakish angle, but he was always respected by all his employees for his integrity. Another gent who invariably wore a hat was Aiden Ward, the Rector of Louth. Altough his hat looked battered, crumpled and wellworn as he cycled through the town, often humming hymns. For all Canon Ward's eccentricity, at least he was a Christian vicar!

The problem at that time was that there were few jobs in Louth to attract the young, which meant that many able and gifted school leavers were forced to look elsewhere for work. In some respects it is the same today; unless you want to become an estate agent, auctioneer, solicitor or accountant, there are still few opportunities.

The worrying part about this book is that the vast majority of people contained within these pages are now dead. For some unknown reason it has never bothered me before having compiled a number of these books. However, on this occasion, flicking through the pages their images now stare out at me like ghosts and it is difficult to believe that so many of them are lying six feet under. A visitor to Louth (an Irish gentleman), who had lived his life in the hustle and bustle of London and Leeds and who rarely visited the countryside, was to remark "Louth reminds me of a preview of the life hereafter!" Perhaps he was right, maybe Louth is an example of the paradise yet to come?

LOUTH
The Twentieth Century

1900 The relief of Mafeking on 19th May may have taken place thousands of miles away in South Africa but it was commemorated in Goulding's Bookshop window, Louth. Images of Baden-Powell as the stalwart hero who outwitted the Boers placed him in a position of prominence. The Goulding family did much to promote literacy in Louth both through Murdie's Select Library and with their printing works on the top floor of this building.

1901 Arthur Hardey Worrall was born in Nottingham in 1868, the son of Robert Worrall. He was educated at Kings School, Grantham, and St John's, Oxford, being appointed Headmaster of Louth Grammar School for Boys in 1901. He attained the rank of captain in the 3rd Volunteer Battalion of the Lincolnshire Regiment (see pages 10 and 11) and was responsible for moulding the Grammar School Cadet Corps.

1902 Worrall was keen on sport and physical exercise. This was the high jump (circa 1902) but what is so interesting is the old thatched cricket pavilion in the background. It wasn't until the arrival of Mr E. A. Gardiner after the First World War that it would be renewed. Indeed, Gardiner's pavilion lasted until the 1990's when an act of vandalism burnt it down.

King Edward VI Grammar School, Louth. The Cadet Corps. 1907.

Worrall's success can be seen here in a display by King Edward VI Grammar School Cadet Corps, photographed in 1907.

Before students could enter the Grammar school there was a choice of schools. This was the British School situated in Kidgate under the headmastership of Mr. Trewick (it is now known as Kidgate).

1903 On 11th June the Great Louth Walking Match took place, with 46 starters.

This same year there was a cycle race. Here we see the competitors being steadied by volunteers before the race.

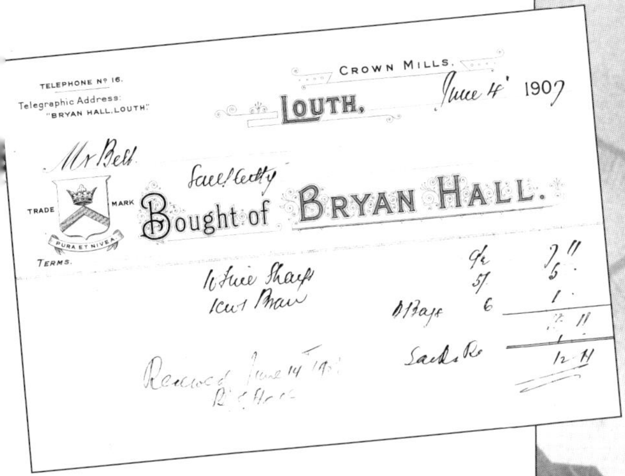
TELEPHONE Nº 16.
Telegraphic Address:
"BRYAN HALL, LOUTH."
CROWN MILLS,
LOUTH, June 4' 1907
Mr Bell
TRADE MARK
PURA ET NIVEA
Bought of BRYAN HALL.
TERMS.
1 cwt Bran
Sacks Re
Received June 14

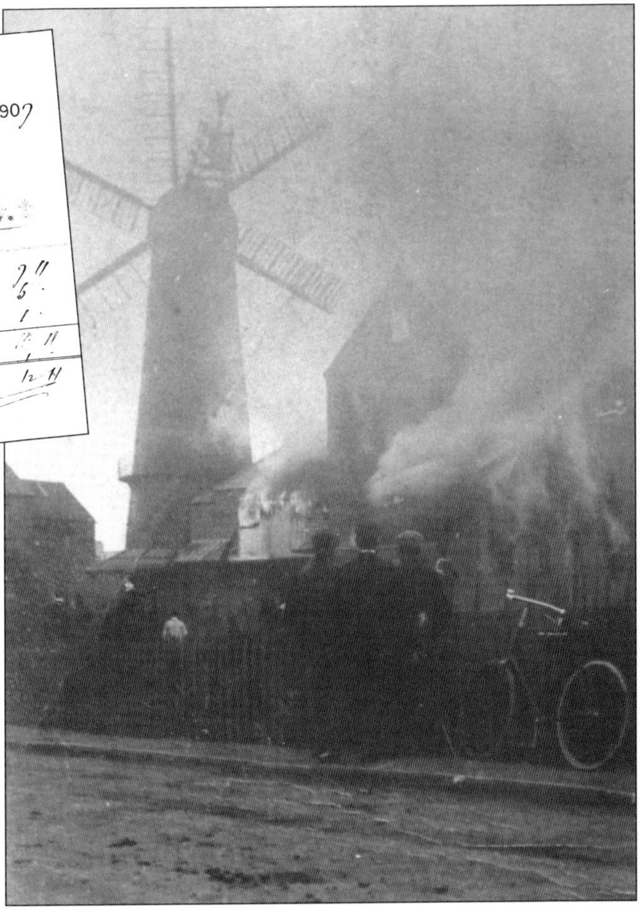

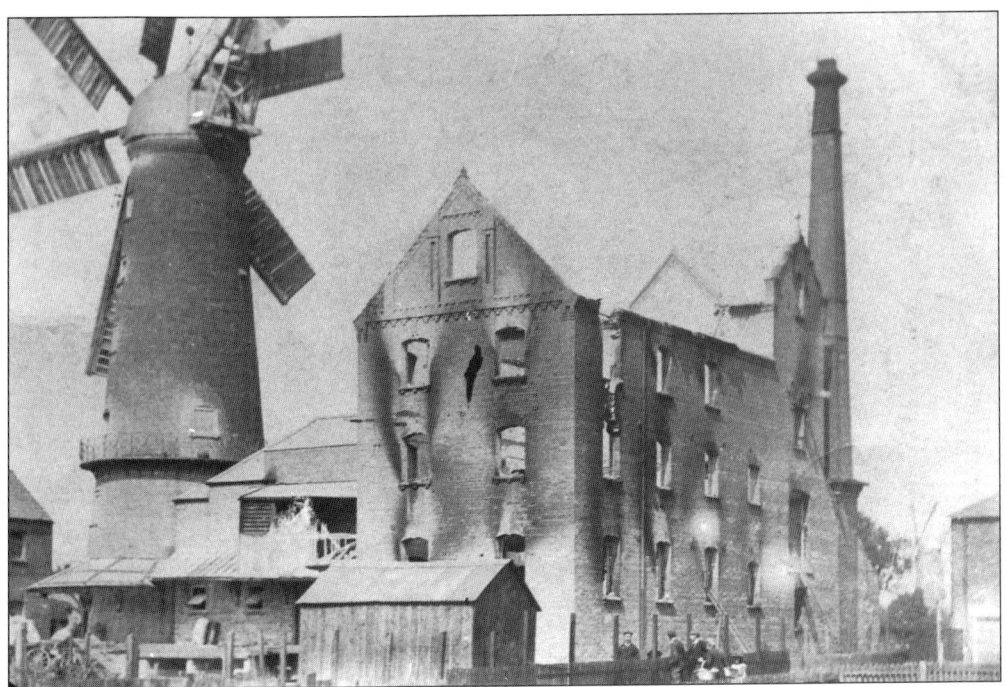

1905 This year Bryan Hall's mill caught fire when a bearing that should have been watered down was left to smoulder. The ensuing fire gutted the building completely.

This was the 3rd Battalion, Lincolnshire Regiment, on parade at Elkington Camp 1905, wearing uniforms more befitting the Boer War.

12   LOUTH The Twentieth Century

1905 Also in this year, General William Booth (1829-1912) arrived in Louth to give a stirring address, as he did in so many towns and cities up and down England. The venerable old religious leader was the founder and first General of the Salvation Army.

1906 Sir Robert Perks (Liberal) was returned as MP for Louth with a majority of 979. This gave Perks the distinction of being the only living Liberal to sit in four successive Parliaments for a Lincolnshire county constituency from 1892-1910. Perks stepped down as M.P. for Louth when he opposed Lloyd George's policy to increase income tax in the 1909 Budget. He was succeeded by Brackenbury the Tory candidate in 1910 who beat the new Liberal candidate Timothy Davies into second place.

In 1906 Lord Baden-Powell arrived in Louth to donate a bust which he had made of Captain John Smith (a distant relative - or so he believed at that time) to Louth Grammar School. He returned in 1909 to inspect his newly-formed group of Boy Scouts in Hubbards Hills (seen here).

1907 The official opening of Hubbards Hills was a momentous occasion. Nearly the entire town turned out to witness the spectacle - a total of 8,000-9,000 people out of Louth's population of 9,518 persons.

14 LOUTH The Twentieth Century

1908 Mahatma Ghandi visited Louth for the second time. The first time he visited his friend and agent, Mr West, of Church Street, in 1906 and the second time in 1908 when he dropped the son of a friend off at Louth Grammar School. His visit was remembered by Ludensians chiefly because the majority of them had never seen a coloured man before.

This was what Louth Station looked like (circa 1908). It was one of the most elegant architectural railway stations in Lincolnshire.

1908 St James' Boys Athletics Club practising on the site of what would become the Wilde Hall and, later still, Northgate Court.

1908 Boys from the British School, Louth, line up to have their photograph taken. No doubt inspired by tales of Empire and spurred on by the *Boys' Own* fantasy of heroism and courage, they were (front row, l to r): Perfect, Vickers, Hosier, Barker, Smith, Langley, Hall, Tomlinson and Smalley, whilst the back row (l to r) were: F. Maudron, Handley, Jarvis, Beard, Wilkinson, Beard, Goodhall and D. Mauldron.

16   LOUTH The Twentieth Century

1909 The Lincolnshire Show came to Louth in 1909. There was an elaborate sign over the entrance to Ramsgate and one in Upgate (seen here), at the junction with South Street which is currently a traffic light operated junction.

At the 1909 Lincolnshire Show was C. G. Smith's Soap Works stand (seen here). The event was held off the Horncastle Road and I can almost smell C. G. Smith's carbolic (they made candles as well) because I grew up with it. Their works were situated in what is now Church Close, Louth, and they sold soft soap for two shillings a bucket - as can be seen in this photograph.   AJ

1909 The Market Place was decorated for the event. The original cobblestones, gas lamp and obelisk water pump are visible, as indeed is Ashton's shop, Strawson's on the corner and Waterloo House. Eventually the Lincolnshire Show was to purchase its own site to use as a showground in 1958.

1910 St James' choir with Canon Wilde, the Rector, seated in the centre. He is surrounded by Reverends Bleazley, Beazor and Bunch, with the organist, Owen Price. The Wilde Hall, now demolished, which was on the site of Northgate Court, was named after him. This same year on 15th January, David Lloyd George was heckled by irate residents and overzealous suffragettes when he addressed Ludensians in Louth Town Hall. He was forced to leave by a side exit. AJ

1911 These elaborate bill-heads, two of which are dated 1911 and addressed to a Mr W. Jacklin, were part of an age when elegance combined with good manners helped to oil the wheels of business. Although still existent in the fifties, they are now part of history. The following year the Titanic was sunk by an iceberg on April 16th, 1912.

1913 On Empire Day there was a march past through the town with every force imaginable showing off their colours. This included the Boy Scouts recently formed and boys from the British Legion. Curiously enough it coincided with one of the most tragic stories of British exploration. Captain Scott's ill-fated polar expedition party were found frozen dead on February 11th.

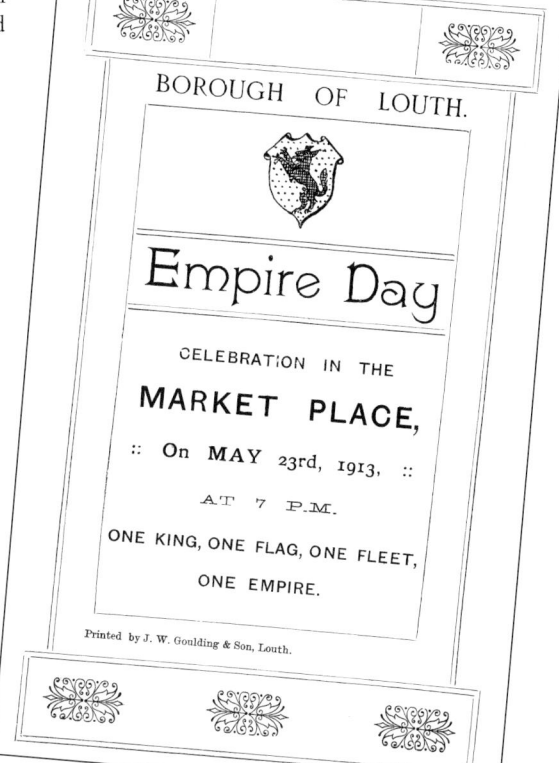

The proceedings came to a close in the evening in the Market Place, when there was an address by the Mayor and Saluting the Flag. Hymns and songs sung included "Oh God, our help in ages past", "The Children's Song" (by Rudyard Kipling), "Land of my Fathers" and "The Roast Beef of Old England". The proceedings ended with three cheers for His Majesty the King.

1913 This was another portion of the procession showing the postmen (bottom left) and firemen.

Away from the pomp and ceremony, this was "A" Squad, 1st Louth Troop, Lincolnshire Yeomanry, going through a cavalry exercise at Louth Camp in 1912.

LOUTH The Twentieth Century

1914 E. C. Woods, the photographer, took this family portrait of a cavalry soldier and family.

RAMSGATE HOUSE STUDIO,
Established 1875
High Class Photography
SPECIALITIES :—
Post Cards, Cabinets, Groups.

NOTE.—Under the Shops Act the Studio is open on THURSDAY Afternoons and closed after 1 p.m. Saturdays.

E. C. WOODS,
Ramsgate House Studio, Louth

Whilst this was Woods' advert. He took over Ramsgate House studio.

1915 Private H. L. ("Les") Howe photographed in 1915 (aged 18) serving with the 5th Lincolnshire Regiment and proudly displaying his famous Sphinx cap-badge. He fought on Messines Ridge and was invalided out of the war effort in 1916.

BRITISH RED CROSS SOCIETY.
TOWN HALL, LOUTH.
A GRAND POPULAR CONCERT
WILL BE HELD ON
THURSDAY, Sept. 27th, 1917,
At 7 p.m., in Aid of
" Our Day " Fund

The following Artistes have kindly promised to help :—Mrs. Hugh Clave, Miss Phyllis Cordeaux, Miss Nellie Robinson, Miss Winch, Miss Yates, Paymaster R. B. Back, Mr. E. A. Gardiner, Mr. Burt Godsmark, Mr. Vernon Howard, Mr. W. Edge, Mr. T. M. Winch, Miss Amy E. Wyld, L.R.A.M., A.R.C.M., and others.

ADMISSION. including Tax :—Reserved Seats, 1/8, Balcony Reserved (First 3 Rows) 1/8. Second Seats and Gallery 1/2, Back Seats 7d. Doors Open at 6-30 Early Doors at 6-15, 3d. extra to the unreserved seats.

TICKETS may be procured of Mr. PARKER, Market Place, or of Mr. BURT GODSMARK.

The Plans of the room are at Mr. C. PARKER'S
N.B.—FULL MOON ON THIS DATE.

1917 On 27th September "A Concert" was held in the Town Hall with Mrs Hugh Clave, Miss Phyllis Cordeaux, Miss Nellie Robinson, Miss Winch, Miss Yates, Paymaster R. B. Back, Mr E. A. Gardiner, Mr Burt Godsmark, Mr Vernon Howard, Mr W. Edge, Mr T. M. Winch, Miss Amy Wyld and others appearing as the artistes.

1918 This was Sgt G. M. Hall of the Royal Engineers, photographed in April 1918. He was one of the lucky ones to return.

1919 Nurse Page was part of the popular Louth troupe known as "The Alvadoras". Others in the troupe included J. J. Wiggen, Maxwell Goodwin, Marian Gell and Les Howe. People had to devise their own entertainment soirees and sing-along parties in front parlours were commonplace. LH

1920 On the 29th May, due to a sudden downpour, the River Lud overflowed and a gushing torrent hit the town. The Louth flood was undoubtedly the worst disaster to befall the town in this century. The extent of the damage can be seen in this view of James Street.

And in these two views of Ramsgate, the devastation (a much maligned word) can also be seen. "Hut Town" was erected off High Holme Road to cope with the homeless.

The hapless Mr G. Berry, who lost three children in the house directly behind him.

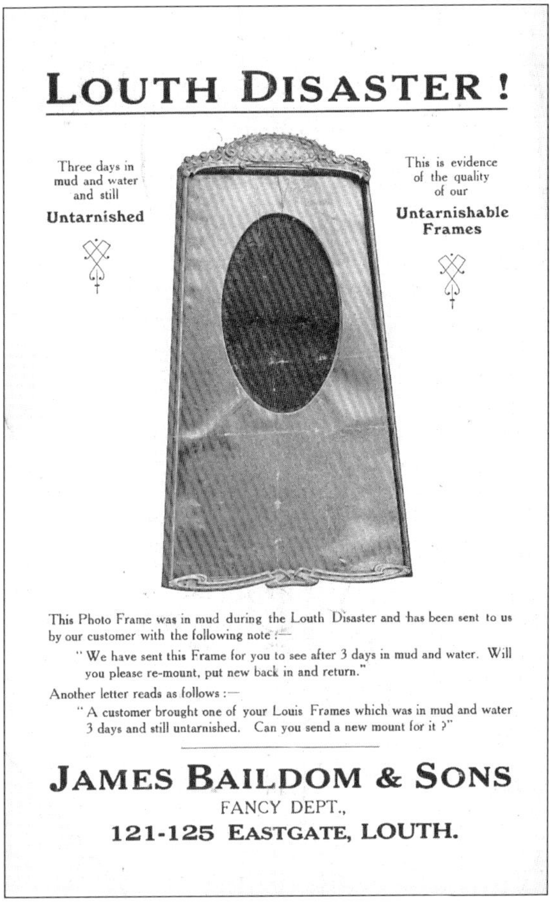

1921 After the flood, many Ludensians tried to pick up the pieces and get on with life. Amongst the many muddy and water-ridden objects was this untarnished picture frame which had survived for three days in the silt! The firm of James Baildom & Sons was quick to seize on the fact.

1921 This was the view of the Golden Fleece yard, photographed by Les Howe. Eventually, when F. W. Woolworth was to buy the old hotel frontage which faced Mercer Row, the present Golden Fleece pub was erected in this yard.
LH

26   L O U T H   T h e   T w e n t i e t h   C e n t u r y

1922 This was a group of employees of the Louth Motor Body Works, photographed in 1922 outside their Ramsgate Road works (now Hi-Lite Signs) just before their annual summer outing.

1925 This was Junior III class at the Girls' Grammar School, 25th June 1925.

1925 Louth Cricket Club were pictured outside their pavilion at the London Road ground. From left to right, back row, they were: W. North (umpire), J. Stubbs, G. E. F. Smith, C. T. Cummings, H. Potts, H. J. Walter (scorer); seated: A. Dexter, D. G. Coney, C. W. V. Webb, W. A. Surfleet, L. J. Harrison, A. J. Towle (groundsman); front row: C. Ives and R. W. Payne.

1924 This same ground was used for the Hospital Cup Final. (This is the 1924 game).

LOUTH EISTEDDFOD

This is to Certify

that H. L. Howe

obtained the Second Prize in the

Photographic Competition

Maximum No. of Marks - Marks obtained -

Number of Entries -

W. B. Kerling. Adjudicators

L. Sowby

C. Hutchinson Hon. Secs.

1926.

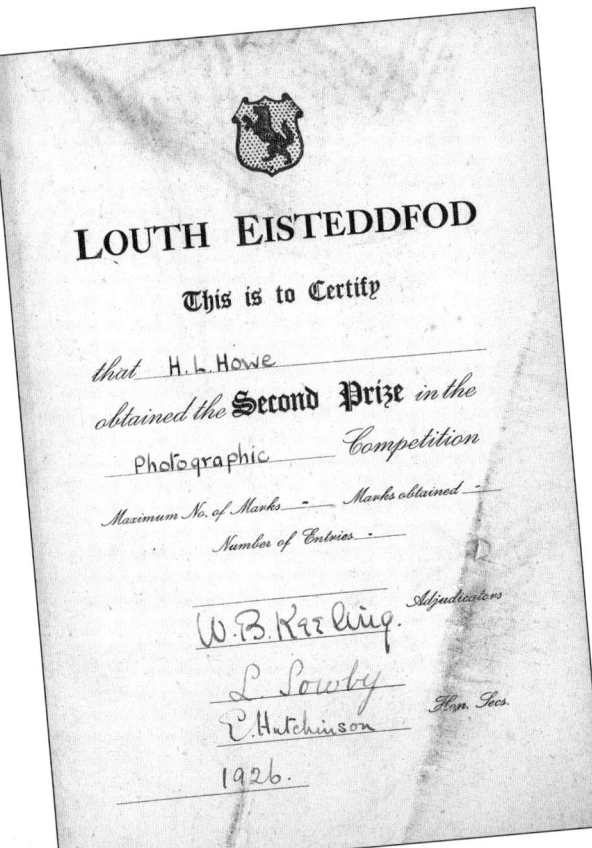

1926 Les Howe's certificate for winning second prize in the photographic competition at the Louth Eisteddfod (he won second prize in 1927 too!). The Louth Eisteddfod, based on the Welsh idea, was to run throughout the twenties and one of the judges was a young Malcolm Sargent from Stamford (then unknown), who later achieved fame with the "Last Night of the Proms".

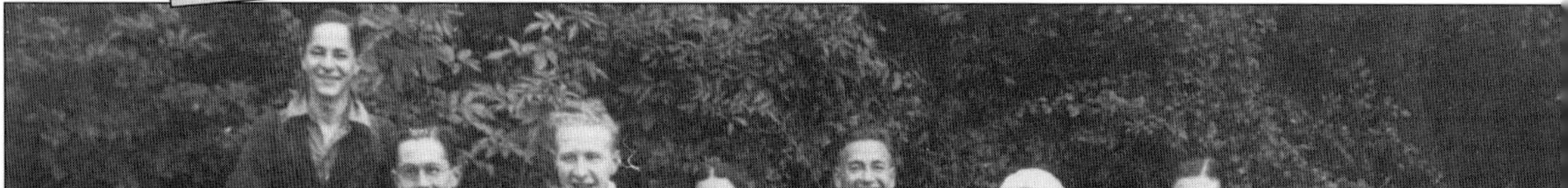

1926 Louth Rambling Club was formed by Mr D. Enderby (seen here in the centre of the group, dressed in a checked pullover).

1927 On 14th June, Princess Helena Victoria came to Louth to open the new extension of Crowtree Lane Hospital (Princess Helena Victoria's mother was one of Queen Victoria's daughters). It was the first time that royalty had ever visited Louth in the 20th century on an official engagement. LH

1924 Bateson's swimming baths were opened on July 17th, 1924 by Dr H. S. Walker and Professor Hobson Bocock. The idea came from Mr Bateson (senior), the local wholesale newsagent, and it ran as a successful private enterprise until the Second World War. Built on the site of a local brewery (an assortment of old bottles was dug up during excavation work and some proved quite valuable), the baths were situated in Church Street (formerly called Maiden Row). They were fed by local spring water but Mr Bateson designed a device for heating this ice cold water which made swimming more acceptable. LH

THE LOUTH & NORTH LINCOLNSHIRE ADVERTISER, ALFORD, MABLETHORPE & SUTTON-ON-SEA TIMES, SATURDAY, JUNE 18, 1927.

Princess Helena at Louth Hospital. Photos of the Event.

Medical and Surgical Staff.

Presenting Princess with Gold Key.—"Daily Chronicle" Copyright.

The Princess conversing with Mrs. H. Stanley Walker.
—"Daily Chronicle" Copyright.

Happy Group of Red Cross Nurses.—"Daily Chronicle" Copyright.

THE PRESIDENT.

Major J. St. Vigor Fox (President).

The Princess shaking hands with the Mayor.
—"Daily Chronicle" Copyright.

The Princess (right), Bishop of Lincoln (left), Matron and Lady-in-Waiting (centre).

Princess and Matron.—"Daily Chronicle" Copyright.

1927 Princess Helena arrived at Little Grimsby Hall (the home of Mrs. Winteringham) on 13th June and travelled to Louth the following day. This same year Stanley Baldwin visited Louth briefly on his way to Hainton Hall.

1927 And Louth Cricket Club again. This time the photograph was taken in front of the stand. This stand, which was situated on almost the same spot as the present Louth Sports Hall, was removed to Horncastle Road. In 1927, from left to right (back row) they were G. H. Ashton (Treasurer), G. Berry, G. N. Fridlington, R. W. Payne, K. Botterill, R. Chatterton, H. Potts and W. North. Front row: J. Stubbs, Capt. C. W. V. Webb (who was friendly with the great Jack Hobbs), W. G. Surfleet (Captain), E. E. Hammond, J. C. Taylor and, in the front, A. Dexter.

1928 Miss Nalder was Headmistress of the Girls' Grammar School and was remembered for her Cheltenham Ladies' College ways and strict discipline.

1928 January saw a young Rowland Hall win first prize in the Town Hall for his version as a young German soldier (see page 41) in the Fancy Dress Ball. These children's parties often tried the patience of Ludensian mothers not only to create imaginative designs but also their talents as potential seamstresses! BR

1928 Electric light was installed in the Market Hall. Presumably it had been lit by gas lamps prior to that date. The problem of lighting, and all those glass panels, may account for its resemblance to a Victorian railway station.

"Banana Bob" on the Fish Shambles, photographed in 1928, was a feature of the town for many years. In the background is the old "Marquis of Granby" pub which has long been demolished.

1929 Donald Pleasance (1919-1995), the actor, attended Monks Dyke School from 1929 to 1933. Although he never returned to the school, years later he sent a tape admitting that he was the culprit who removed the missing canes from the teachers' common room. Donald and his brother, Ralph, who also attended Monks Dyke, travelled to school and back by train from Grimoldby Station, where their father was Station Master. On the day in question, Donald Pleasance rode in the cab of the locomotive en route between Louth and Grimoldby and threw the offending canes into the train's firebox. He is seen here in the BBC's version of Trollope's "The Barchester Chronicles".

1929 This photograph was taken shortly after the opening of Monks Dyke School, with Percy Latter on the right of the picture (standing and dressed in a light grey suit). Also pictured is Mr Cheesman (in a blazer).

1929 In April, the Mountebanks appeared and were photographed for the Louth Standard. This troupe may have inspired the Louth Playgoers to form three years later. In October the crash on Wall Street took place which ruined tens of thousands of small investors and sent reverberations around the world.

1930 There were few motor cars in Louth at this time. This was a Singer Eight belonging to George Hall, (see page 22) photographed at Little Cawthorpe.

1930 On Mayor's Sunday, this was the procession. Front row: Major J. St. Vigor Fox (High Steward); Mayor Bert Appleby (family butcher, of 7-9 Aswell Street, well-known for his pork pies) and H. R. Roberts (Town Clerk). In the background are Col. A. P. Heneage MP, Mr Street and Mr Coney.

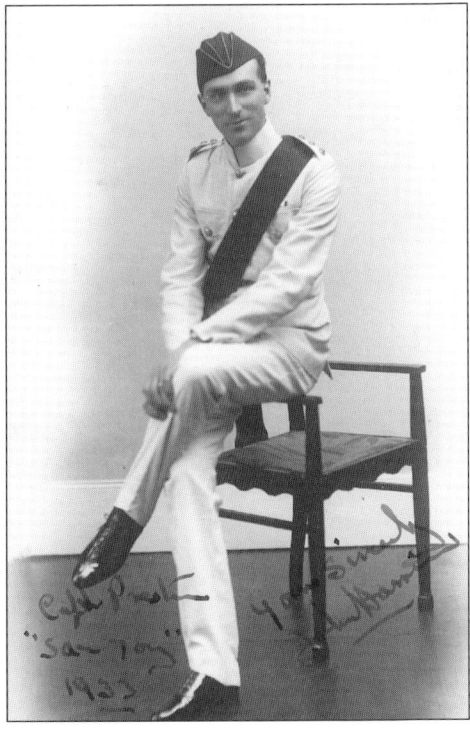

1930's Between 1925 and 1939 the Louth Operatic Society staged some memorable performances, mostly at the Playhouse Cinema. They disbanded at the beginning of World War II. Margaret Godsmark (Rose Marie, 1936), T. H. Foster as "Slinks" (Miss Hook of Holland, 1931), John Harrison as Capt. Preston (San Toy, 1933), Christina Tucker as Katie (Rio Rita, 1937).

Up to 1936 these were works previously produced by the Louth Amateur Operatic Society.

"Pirates of Penzance"	1925
"Yeomen of the Guard"	1926
"Mikado"	1927
"Gondoliers"	1928
"Mountebanks"	1929
"Florodora"	1930
"Miss Hook of Holland"	1931
"Country Girl"	1932
"San Toy"	1933
"Yeomen of the Guard"	1934
"Desert Song"	1935

1936
Louth Amateur Operatic Society
Presents

ROSE MARIE

Souvenir Programme　　　Price 6d.

The *Austin* HERTFORD SALOON with 16 H.P. (Six Cylinder) Engine £298

1936 Models 7 h.p. from £102 - 10 - 0.　10 h.p. from £158.
Delivery from Stock.　　　　　　　　11.9 h.p. from £188.
Several used Cars and Vans in stock, Part exchange, Deferred terms

E. P. TOWLE, Authorised Austin Dealer
Phone 212.　　　　　　　　　NEWMARKET GARAGE, LOUTH.

In the thirties these were E. P. Towle's car prices!

1931 This photograph of Mr Sowerby and Mr Hunter sitting on one of the pig pens was taken about this time. Mr Sowerby became a partner in John Taylor & Sons, whilst Mr Hunter, who lived in Lee Street, died aged 87. He always wore that bowler, starched collar and spoon polished boots. Incidentally, the covered pig market had not been built by this date.

1931 At the 4th Annual Show and Sale of Utility Poultry, held in the Cornmarket on 2nd December, there were Rhode Island Red Pullets, White Whyandotte Pullets, Leghorn Pullets, AOV Pullets, Rhode Island Red Cockerels, White Wyandotte Cockerels, Leghorn Cockerels and AOV Cockerels, which puzzles this author. I had no idea there were so many different types.

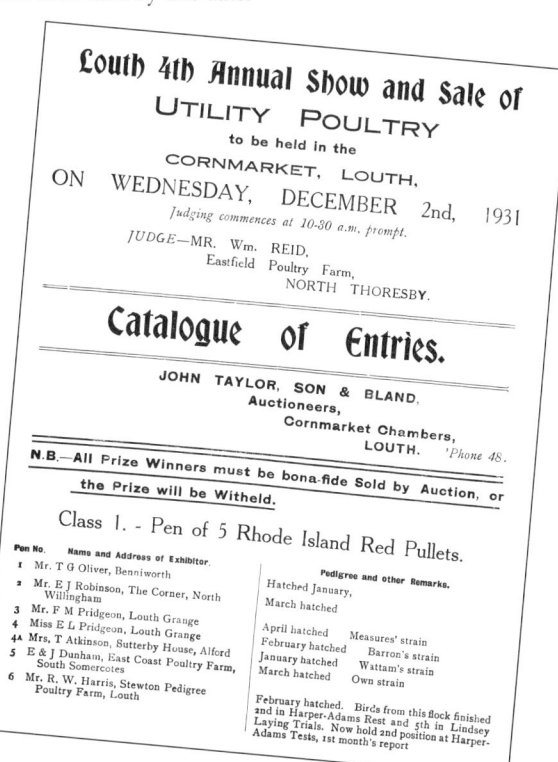

Every year there was a football match held on the London Road Ground with the proceeds going to Louth Hospital (Crowtree Lane). This year it was between Louth and the Royal Air Force.

HOSPITAL CUP FINAL.

LOUTH
(Holders) v.

ROYAL AIR FORCE
By kind permission of the Commanding Officer.

LONDON ROAD GROUND,
ON THURSDAY, APRIL 30th, 1931,

Kick-off 6-30 p.m.

The Entire Proceeds will be handed over to Louth Hospital.

ADMISSION 6D.
[see over

1932 Children's parties were still held in the Town Hall throughout the thirties, no matter which political persuasion, whether Liberal or Tory. This was the Louth Conservative Children's Ball, held on 8th January 1932. In February Sir Malcolm Campbell set a new land speed record in Blue Bird. LH

1932 In the autumn, this photograph of many prominent Louth characters was taken in the Town Hall. Mayor Jesse Rushforth is seated third from left whilst Canon Burton is third from right. Amongst those standing at the back are Hugh Efemey, Dr Laughton-Smith, Arthur Price, Owen Price and George Hall.

1933 On Remembrance Day the gathering which assembled to pay their respects at the War Memorial under the watchful eyes of Mayor Ernest Harry Thompson (he was to become Mayor again in 1940) included, on the extreme left, Lt. Col. Heneage, the Louth MP. Also just visible in the background is "Clare" photographer's studio.

In complete contrast to the light operettas of Louth Operatic Society, Louth Choral Society's programme held on 18th May was much more serious, with Mrs Hammond and Mrs Drinkel as sopranos, Mr Hugh Efemey as tenor, Sydney Smith as baritone and Dr Gordon Slater of Lincoln Cathedral on the organ. The conductor was Mr Owen Price.

LOUTH CHORAL SOCIETY.

– Programme –
OF A

Musical Service

TO BE HELD IN

Louth Parish Church

On Thursday Evening, May 18th, 1933

AT 7 O'CLOCK

"Hymn of Praise" *(Mendelssohn)*
"Blest Pair of Sirens" *(Hubert Parry)*
Cantata No. 82, First Movement *(Bach)*
Andante con moto from 5th Symphony *(Beethoven)*

PRINCIPALS:

Sopranos : Mrs. E. E. HAMMOND
Mrs. H. DRINKEL
Tenor : Mr. H. B. EFEMEY
Baritone : Mr. SYDNEY SMITH
Leader : Miss EVEYLN ALEXANDER (Hull)
Organ : Dr. GORDON SLATER, F.R.C.O.,
(LINCOLN CATHEDRAL)
Conductor : Mr. OWEN M. PRICE, F.R.C.O., L.R.A.M.

CHORUS AND ORCHESTRA OF 100 PERFORMERS

C. Parker & Co., Printers, 19 Market Place, Louth.

1934 Music was encouraged in Louth, firstly through Herbert Tyson of Newmarket who made violins, violas, double-basses and cellos and latterly through Lance Brown whose music shop in Aswell Street stocked an assortment of instruments (mainly brass). This was the music class of Kidgate School with the late Brian Howe on the left of the picture and the late Peter Smith (butcher of Upgate) fourth from left. Peter Smith became Mayor of Louth in 1975.

1934 This photograph of a young Jim Laverack on horseback with his father may have been taken near Lincoln but he was to make a large impact on Louth when he took over the firm of John Taylor & Sons.

1934 On 22nd November Louth Playgoers Society produced "Rookery Nook", the Ben Travers farce, in the Playhouse. Some familiar names took part, including Rita Uzzell (daughter of the Louth Standard's editor, Mr C. W. Uzzell), C. D. Hemming, E. A. Gardiner, C. S. Rowland and Wendy Lill.

1935 Albert Ernest Maxey was Mayor of Louth. Flanked by Major J. St. Vigor Fox and Hughie Roberts, Maxey was to become Mayor in 1935, 1941, 1955 and 1956, accepting the Freedom of the Borough in 1955.

LOUTH The Twentieth Century 45

1935 At the 1935 Children's New Year Ball held at the Town Hall we see a group of youngsters heralding in the New Year with Old Father Time just to the right. LH

1935 May saw the celebration of King George V's Silver Jubilee. Crowds flocked to the Market Place at a time when the county was recovering from the Depression and the economy was trying to kick-start itself into more prosperous times. LH

1935 Bunting and Union Jacks, with an occasional St George's flag thrown in for good measure, adorned the whole town. This was the view of the Cornmarket, with a wonderful display of old cars.   LH

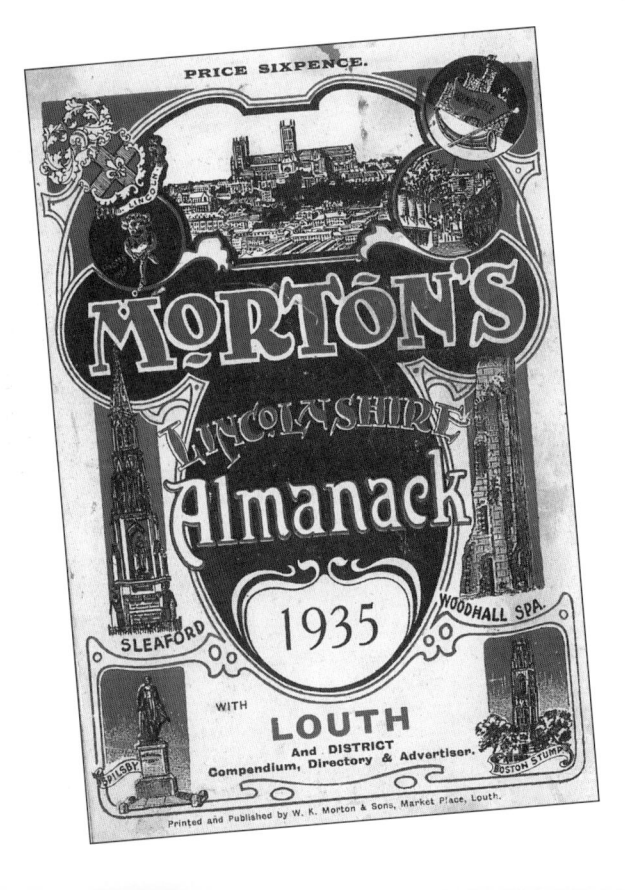

Morton's produced their Louth Almanack in the same vein that Gouldings had done before them. This acted as a sort of telephone directory before telephone directories were thought of with relevant information. The following year King Edward VIII abdicated on December 11th, 1936.

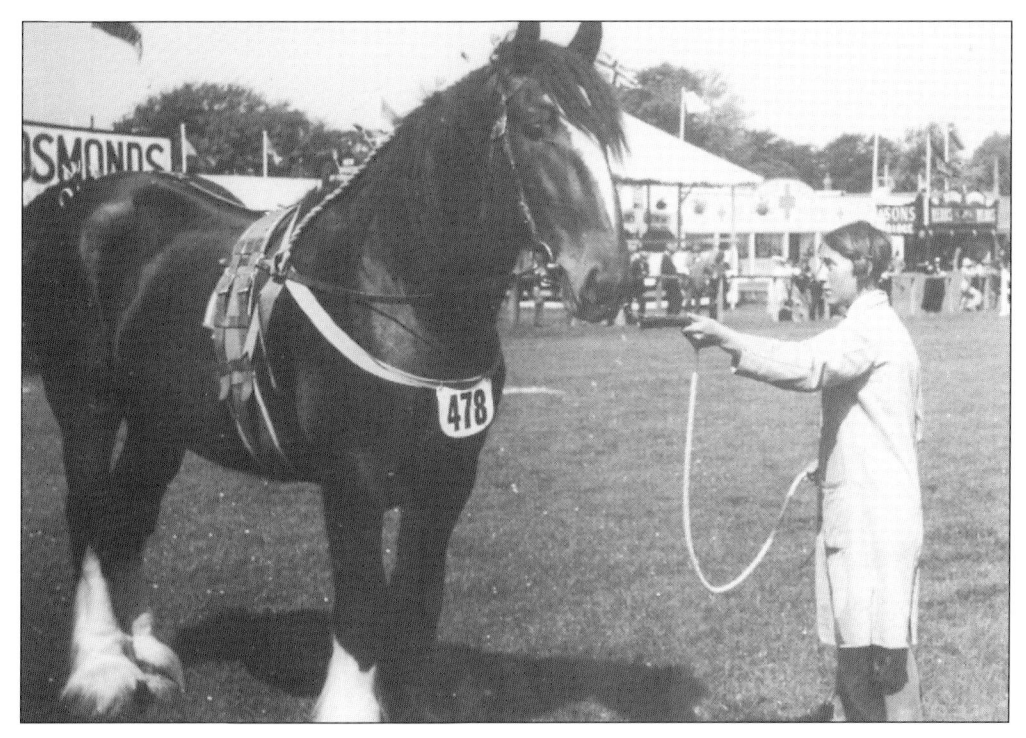

1936 The Lincolnshire Show took place just outside Louth. This was Miss Elvin (daughter of the hairdresser in Upgate) showing off a wonderful shire horse. Miss Elvin is probably best remembered for her Southwold Riding School, which operated out of her Bridge Street stables.

1937 On 13th October Louth's first ever broadcast on the wireless was made from Louth Town Hall. The concert was held as a celebration of the work of Mr H. W. Tyson, the musical instrument maker, of Newmarket, Louth. From left to right, the back row are: Eric Teesdale, Ralph Fytche, Miss Kent, Mrs Satchell, Herbert Tyson, Joyce Towle, George Borman, Walter Barton and George Stevenson. Middle row (standing): Rev. J. Loughton, Mr I. Smith, Mr Kingsland, R. Smith, Alec Meanwell, Catherine Heaton, Reg Smith, John Stovin, Mr L. Dennis, Miss P. Enefer, Eric Rawlings, Maud Bullivant, Herbert Berry and Albert Stanley; (seated) Charles Smith, Charles Briggs, Roy Bullivant, Joyce Rawlings, Doris Briggs, Eileen Stones, Derek Meanwell, Harry Stones, George Lister, Norman Laking and Ernest Lister. Seated in front are: Eileen Bullivant, Norah Watkins, Betty Brock, Madeleine Tyson and Maureen Meanwell. LH

Louth Parish Church.

✠

A Service of Thanksgiving
for the
Restoration of the Tower and Spire of St. James' Church, Louth.
At 7-45 p.m.

Sunday, July 24th, 1938.
Eve of the Patronal Festival.

✠ ✠ ✠

The Service will be broadcast on the National Wave Length.

T. E. WIGGEN & SON LTD., PRINTERS, LOUTH.

1938 On Sunday 24th July there was a Service of Thanksgiving for the restoration of the tower and spire of St James'. The service was broadcast on the radio (National Wavelength) and included an address by the Bishop of Lincoln. The service ended with "Praise my soul, the King of Heaven".

1938 Carnival Night was when the fair came to town and any monies were collected as a benefit in aid of the local Louth hospital in Crowtree Lane. When Louth handed over Crowtree Lane Hospital to the N.H.S. after the war, the town handed over an independent working hospital which had been paid for by sixpences, shillings and coppers collected over a twenty year period.

1939 This was the year when Mrs Eliza Baildom died (Louth's oldest tradeswoman), aged 93. She was the widow of Councillor James Baildom (of the furnishing firm of James Baildom & Son, who died on 14th May, 1930). It was also the year when this wonderful advert appeared: "I'm glad I took your advice. I've been a different woman since I cut out washdays and sent everything to . . . Winton's Laundry, Louth". A well known dog-food factory moved into Winton's Laundry when they vacated the premises.

1939 On 24th December a platoon of the Northumberland Fusiliers were photographed in the Wellington pub yard, led by Captain Lord Hugh Percy (the Duke of Northumberland). They were stationed there for a short time before being sent on active service. The Wellington pub was in a prime position next to the railway so they could be sent at a moment's notice. LH

THE TOWN HALL
LOUTH.

Sunday, 6th October, 1940
at 2-30 p.m. and 7-30 p.m.

"MELODY BANQUET"
A "MELODY" PRODUCTION

Proceeds for the Louth Hospital and the Spitfire Fund

Menu 3d.

The "Melody Makers" included Gibson on drums, Les Hunter on accordian, Geoffrey Howe on guitar and Basil Lock on saxophone. Basil Lock later became an Air-Vice-Marshal in the R.A.F. LH

1940 The programme consisted of the opening chorus, The Melody Makers, Jack Dukes, Three Jolly Housewives, "1966 and all that" (a peep into domestic affairs of 26 years hence), Joyce Parker (one of the county's best singers), That Man Skinner, Driver Hall, I want to be an actor, Ron Appleby (mostly on accordion), the tenor John Harrison, Soft Lights and Sweet Melody, G. D. M. Wood (who got things done) and the yodeller G. N. R. Fittes.

1940 The railway soon adopted its company of Home Guard volunteers (they were formed in September 1940). Here we see a lesson in throwing hand grenades. By December all the men of 16 Platoon, D Company, 9th Lindsey Battalion, had been issued with boots, great-coats, uniforms, gaiters and bayonets and the following year they were inspected by Lt Gen Eastwood, GOC Northern Command.

1940 Another company of Home Guard was 17 Platoon, D Company, 9th Lindsey Battalion, whose Commanding Officer was Col. Oscar Dixon (seated, second row, fifth from left). This same year 335,000 troops were taken off Dunkirk and transported home. It was a miracle. LH

1941 This was Louth's answer to the concert party featured in "It 'ain't 'alf hot, Mum". They entertained the troops and the RAF, often visiting farms or aerodromes under blackout conditions. It meant that their drivers had to have excellent eyesight, quick reactions and know the road. The concert party consisted of; from left to right, Hugh Efemey (tenor), Daisy Lee (singer), Sydney Platt (pianist), Reg Cash (comedian), Cyril Holland (the butt of the jokes and nicknamed "Our Enoch"), Reg Smith (comedian and violinist), Sydney Smith (baritone), Jessie Ainger (singer) and B. Carter Eastwood (who sang and played the ukelele).

1945 8th May was VE Day (Victory in Europe) an Bert Hallam's Ideal Home in St Mary's Lane was decorated for the event. Now known as Brenton Lodge, this was once one of the best examples of art deco in the county. It has been altered so much over the years by various owners that it i almost unrecognisable today.

Bert ("Bertie") Hallam, who owned the Playhouse Cinema, encouraged local group such as the Louth Operatic Society and the Playgoers to perform at his theatre. He was also responsible for producing local newsreels depicting events and happenings in the town which are now considered archive material.

Daily Mirror

Wednesday, May 9, 1945
No. 12,912 — ONE PENNY
Registered at G.P.O. as a Newspaper.

MAY 9

BRITAIN'S DAY OF REJOICING

Cheering their "Winnie"

Dense crowds in Whitehall, estimated by the police at 50,000—all cheering like mad—mobbed the Prime Minister when he emerged from Downing-street after his broadcast speech. With the broad grin of victory on his face—and a new cigar clamped between his teeth—Winston Churchill gave his famous V-sign.

Minute past midnight

THE final total surrender documents were signed by the Germans and the three Allies yesterday IN BERLIN. The Channel Isles were to be freed at once. Hostilities in Europe ended officially at 12.1 a.m. today.

1945 This was the front page of the Daily Mirror, which had already become a tabloid long before most of the other newspapers even thought of the idea.

54 LOUTH The Twentieth Century

1945 The Mayor, Councillor William Rowson (the baker), and Mace-bearer Heward photographed at the War Memorial. LH

1946 After the war, housing became a priority. Temporary pre-fabricated homes were erected in Park Avenue, off Eastfield Road, and Mayor and Mrs Shelton (seen here) gave the first occupants their keys. Curiously, these same prefabs are still used to this day and are well-kept. Kneeling in the foreground is Frank MacDonald (with moustache) and Harry Wilcox (with glasses and mackintosh). LH

1947 Louth Town football team. The following year Louth Town and Nats amalgamated to form Louth United. The 1947 team comprised (left to right): Mo Dales, G. Cross, A. Cross, G. Walker, Len Scott, S. Salt, A. Miles, Willoughby and Spittlehouse; (front row) Barton, Richardson, Marland, R. Dann and Reed.

1948 J. H. Elvin, the ladies hairdresser, of Upgate, whose premises Madame Daphne inherited, was a keen rider. This photograph was taken at the Christmas meet of the Southwold Hunt in 1948 at Kenwick Hall. Elvin's daughter shared her father's passion for horses. Meanwhile, thousands of miles away, Mahatma Ghandi was assassinated on 30th January when he was shot four times at close range. LH

A small booklet written by Fred Crosby explaining how the railway arrived in Louth from its conception in 1845 to its first trial run of 7th March 1848. How Miss Pye of The Cedars had laid the foundation stone on 8th July 1847 and the opening of the W. H. Smith & Sons bookstall in 1877.

1848   LOCAL RAILWAY CENTENARY   1948

SOUVENIR OF THE EXHIBITION
at
LOUTH MUSEUM
(Enginegate, near to Town Hall)
MONDAY, 29th MARCH
to
SATURDAY, 3rd APRIL

"STIRLING"
8 ft. Single, built 1895, stationed at Louth, 1912.

PRICE THREEPENCE
Louth Advertiser, Ltd.

1950 The old Malt Kiln next to the railway was bombed in 1940. The new one, which had to be built on the site of the original to obtain war-aid compensation, is under construction in this photograph. Here we see the foundations of the building with the old cottages on Newbridge Hill, which were in turn demolished to make way for the Lin Pac factory.   LH

1951 Brampton College, Louth, was on the site of what is now Douglas Electronics on Eastfield Road. A young Stuart McLeod is seated on the front row (extreme left).

Also this year (1951) saw the debut of "Bill and Ben" (the flowerpot men) broadcast on Radio's "Listen with Mother". They were the invention of Hilda Brabban (headmistress of Eastfield Road Infants School) and were later transferred to the BBC television's "Watch with Mother". Hilda Brabban's daughter married the Rt. Rev. Neville Chamberlain.

1952 And Louth had a railway station. This was a familiar sight as some folk set off down to London. One gentleman, dressed in a bowler and shiny polished shoes, even used to commute to London each day on the old Louth to London line.

MEN AND WOMEN OF LOUTH WHO GAVE THEIR LIVES DURING THE SECOND WORLD WAR 1939–1945

BARRY C. ARLISS	ALBERT LANCASTER
FRANK G. ARLISS	WILLIAM E. LANCASTER
KENNETH S. ARNOLD	W. KEITH MORTON
DOUGLAS E. AYRE	STANLEY MUMBY
JAMES BARTON	JACK NEALE
W. KENNETH BARTON	JACK NEWSOME
EDWARD B. BLACKBURN	MAURICE R. NUTT
CHARLES J. BLACKMAN	WALTER OAKES
ALFRED BLADES	GEORGE A. OWEN
P. OLIVER BOWEN	CHARLES R. PARSONS
REGINALD BRATLEY	BRIAN C. PAUL
VINCENT J. BRYANT	EDWARD PHILLIPS
FRANK N. BURGESS	GEORGE E. PICKARD
GEOFFREY R. CHAPMAN	EDWARD PULLING
JOSEPH CLARK	LESLIE C. ROWORTH
ANTHONY W. COLLEY	ERIC E. SCHOLEY
LESLIE COWHAM	ARCHIBALD L. SEARBY
JAMES CRASHLEY	ROBERT P. SMART
JOHN L. CRIBB	HERBERT SMITH
RONALD G. CROW	C. RODNEY SMITH
MAURICE E. DAWSON	JOSEPH STAINTON
RONALD M. DAY	GEORGE STEPHENSON
JACK DRURY	GRAHAM B. STOCKS
GEORGE A. FAULKNER	KENNETH W. SWINGLER
ROY FENWICK	DEREK TACEY
S. ALLEN FORMAN	WILLIAM M. THOMSON
HENRY R. FOXON	RICHARD H. TRAFFORD
CHARLES K. D. FRESHNEY	E. EASTON VERGETTE
CHARLES E. GEE	FRED WADDINGHAM
RICHARD G. GIDDINGS	FREDERICK WAKELIN
I. ROY GRANT	GEORGE R. WALMSLEY
REGINALD HALLAM	REGINALD WEST
ARTHUR HANSON	GEORGE E. WHITWORTH
GEORGE H. HAW	RONALD G. WILLERTON
ROBERT E. HEWINS	FREDERICK W. YOUNGER
RICHARD B. HEWSON	MARGARET REED
CHARLES R. HOWDEN	BRENDA I. WELLS
ALFRED E. L. JULLIEN	MAY JOHNSON
FRANK KING	

1952 On 12th October the Louth and District Branch of the Royal British Legion held a service at the War Memorial to the men and women of Louth who gave their lives during the Second World War (1939-1945). The memorial tablets were unveiled by Major the Rt Hon The Earl of Ancaster, Lord Lieutenant of Lincolnshire and County Patron of the Royal British Legion.

The Eastfield brothers (above) played the last post at the War Memorial for many years.

The tradition is held to this day, as this photograph of 11th November 1991 bears testimony. At the head of this group on its way to the War Memorial is the late Phyllis West (dressed in hat). But once again many of this group have since passed away.

1953 Nearly every street in Louth had its own shop at one time. In the fifties and sixties many small corner shops were forced to close. This was E. A. Lowis's newsagents and tobacconists in Little Eastgate which was sold to Lenton Ottaway by John Taylor, Stennett & Stevenson on Tuesday 1st October, 1953.

1953 The year started badly on 31st January with the East Coast Floods. Louth acted as an emergency relief centre and one woman, Mrs L. Ball of Tennyson Avenue, Mablethorpe, refused to be transported to Louth because she had lost her home in the Louth Flood of 29th May 1920 and did not want to be reminded of the fact. She was evacuated to Alford instead. GET

This was Mablethorpe!

1953 After the floods, Wilfred Pickles brought his "Have a Go" team to cheer up the beleaguered inhabitants of Mablethorpe. Before he left Lincolnshire he appeared briefly at the Louth Playhouse and was mobbed, such was the popularity of his radio programme. The late Wilfred Pickles is survived today by the controversial Judge Pickles and his granddaughter is a successful actress. BR

1953 But, as the year wore on, things got better: on 3rd June Queen Elizabeth II was crowned in Westminster Abbey. Everyone dived into everyone else's front room and watched the event on television. Street parties abounded - this was the one in High Holme Crescent, when sticky buns, sandwiches and lashings of lemonade were doled out on trestle tables. LH

1953 In the autumn, a boxing contest was held in the Town Hall. The Socialist Mayor Frank Macdonald, who was also Mayor of Louth in 1973 and 1979, won his bout. It would be another forty years before the next boxing contest would be held in the Town Hall. BR

1953 Cyril Osborne also had a fight on his hands this year with the Labour candidate, Mr Poirrer. Seen here winning the election we see Cyril Osborne (who was MP from 1945 until his death in 1969), his wife (centre) and daughter (right), with the loser, Mr and Mrs Poirrer. BR

1954 Some members of the original Louth Athletics Club jogging along Crowtree Lane, Louth. It is possible to recognise Derek Turner, Wilf Charlton, Kirkham and Tom Barton. This same year Roger Bannister ran his 4 minute mile. BR

1954 At the Business & Professional Women's Club dinner, Mrs E. H. Gasking (Chairman of Batchelors Peas) was the guest speaker. She inherited the position at the age of 22 on the death of her father and during her 25 years in business watched the company grow from a family to a national concern. Also present at the dinner were the Mayoress, Mrs W. R. Burr, Cyril Osborne MP and Councillor R. E. West. BR

1954 At the Rotary Club dinner, the first three well-known characters are (from left to right): Stan Shone, Basil Sharpley (the former Coroner), Mr R. Sandwith (who bought Eve & Ranshaw) and Mr R. Brackenbury (who became Mayor of Louth in 1958 and 1969). BR

In October these delegates were sent to the Conservative Party Conference, Blackpool. They were (l to r), back row: Major Clixby Fitzwilliams (Healing), Mr Tom Grimoldby (Cleethorpes, Alexandra Ward); middle row: Miss B. L. Hamley (Divisional Agent) and Mrs Clixby Fitzwilliams; front: Mrs G. H. Wilcox.
BR

Rev. Ward

"The Spire" magazine, with its editorial by Rev. Aiden Ward (Rural Dean) was St James' parish news. Bishop Harland was Bishop of Lincoln (1947-1956) and the view on the cover shows Upgate as it used to be.

THE SPIRE

DECEMBER, 1954   THREEPENCE

1955 Two great characters of Louth, "Jack" Yates (President of Louth Antiquarian & Naturalists Society) and Mr Robinson, the fruit and nurseryman, receiving a plate clock. "Jack" Yates (real name, Theodore) was a confirmed bibliophile who bought Gouldings bookshop in 1948 and ran it until 1960 when his manager, Vernon Guy-Knight bought the business.   BR

Mayor Albert Ernest Maxey with his back to the camera is watching the march past. BR

GRENADIER GUARDS ASSOCIATION
(Louth Sub Branch).

FIRST ANNUAL BALL
in The Town Hall, Louth,
FRIDAY, FEBRUARY 25th, 1955
Dancing 8 p.m. to 2 a.m.
Licensed Bar 8 p.m to 1 a.m.
REGIMENTAL DANCE BAND
OF THE GRENADIER GUARDS
By kind permission of
Colonel T. F. C. Winnington, M.B.E.,
Lt. Colonel Commanding the Regiment

TICKETS   (including supper)   15/-

The Grenadiers found Louth a lucrative recruiting ground for ambitious young men who wanted a career in the forces.
BR

1955 A group of Louth Girl Guides photographed in July, with Miss Cordeaux standing at the back in the centre. Phyllis Cordeaux wrote "Moonlight and Shadow" (a collection of poems) published in 1926 by Heath Cranton of London. Louth's newest school, off-High Holme Road was to be named Cordeaux High School. On 14th May 1955 it was about three or four months behind schedule and the eventual cost was over £100,000 (a considerable sum in the fifties). BR

1955 One feature in the fifties was the old people's tea held in Legbourne similar to the Mid-Marsh parties. The one below was also held in 1955; Mr Pitt and Dr Walker's son are recognisable. BR

1956 Throughout the fifties the winters were bleak and white with sharp frosts, although none of them compared with the winter of '47. This was the scene in January 1956 on Welton-le-Wold top with two local drivers having to shovel their way through the drifts of snow.

1956 This was a Post Office presentation at the "Lincolnshire Poacher". It has always been traditional to give some gift or memento when anyone retires, but why is it nearly always a clock?   BR

1956 October - the Louth Chrysanthemum Fayre in aid of St James' £50,000 appeal. Mrs Maple Bedford (formerly Maple Marfleet) and Mrs Nielson took charge of the bottle stall as they had done the previous year. BR

1958 Hedley Warr (1899-1978), seated second from left, with G. R. Hobbs the master on his right and a group of Grammar School boys. This was taken shortly before Warr's retirement in 1958: he was Headmaster of the Grammar School (1941-1958). LH

1959 On 6th February "Les" Howe died in Louth County Hospital. My favourite photograph of his was the policeman on traffic duty at the junction of Upgate with Mercer Row. It somehow summed up his life, which was simple, uncomplicated and honest and he portrayed it as such. How he would have fared in our present society when even the simplest task seems to be difficult, I hate to think. Although I never spoke to him, I remember seeing him walking around the town with the inevitable camera over his shoulder in a purposeful manner. All these years later I realise why.

72 LOUTH The Twentieth Century

The aerial view of Eastgate and Eastfield Road was taken in 1959. Note Holy Trinity Church in the foreground, which burnt down in 1991. The council houses in St Bernard's Avenue look relatively established (they were built in the early fifties) and the Lincolnshire Poacher (formerly Park House) looks gleaming - it was Louth's newest pub/hotel in 1953! Louth Swimming Pool had not been built and nor had Old Mill Park.

LOUTH The Twentieth Century 73

1960 Barton's grocery store on Newmarket was to receive a new frontage. This was the old shop with its adverts for the Playhouse and Palace cinemas. Incidentally, the owner was given a free pass for displaying these signs.

Whilst this was the interior, where Tom Barton could dispense slices of bacon along with other grocery items. Supermarkets had not infiltrated Louth's grocery trade by this date.

1961 Lin Pac started from humble beginnings in 1959 (the brainchild of Mr Cornish) to become the internationally renowned company it is today. In September 1961 a new £100,000 corrugating machine was installed in Charles Street (at the time it was called the Lincolnshire Packaging Company). The machine was operating within three weeks of its arrival, largely due to the excellent work of Macdonald's Engineers and the help of Mr H. Kirby, the electrician. "The rest is history", as they say. Curiously the same site had been used by the Louth Wallpaper factory, the Louth Arrota Works and latterly as a canning factory.

1962 Louth Cricket Club was 140 years old (established 1822). The team winning the Bale Cup and photographed in front of the by now old pavilion (built 1934) comprised (back row, left to right): Keith Sizer, Dick Butler, Colin Johnson, Gordon Alrich, Les Hunter and Colin Hounsome. Front row: Mary Papworth, B. Cook, J. Riggall, M. Lee, B. Papworth, B. Bosworth and George Gunther. It was in August of this year that Marilyn Monroe died.

1962 Mr Stevenson, the auctioneer, of John Taylor's, talking to Ted Moult, the farmer and TV/radio personality, in Louth Town Hall at the annual Farmers' Dinner.

1964 The big story of the year was the disappearance of Vernon Guy-Knight. His Jaguar car was found at the Randolph Hotel in Oxford but there was no sign of him. Because of his disappearance Goulding's bookshop would close after 277 years in business. J. W. Goulding had bought the business, back in 1886, and Jack Yates bought it in 1948 after the death of the last Miss Goulding. Guy Vernon-Knight was the last owner.

1966 On 11th June the judges at the Elkington Show were, from left to right, Eric Ranby of Grimblethorpe, Gilbert Smith and "Walt" Bett of Hainton. It is Julie Barton on the horse in the background.

1966 Mr Burgess' class, Kidgate School, taken in the Autumn Term. Jeremy Holmes, Janice Brown, Sandra Barnes, Susan Taylor, Nicola Barton and Lynn Blythe are recognisable.

1970 The Crusaders' pantomime in this year included Basil Coxon, Ian Grant, Heather Chatterton, Ann Mountain, Alison Lill (extreme right, seated), Paula Barton with a young Peter Mountain (centre stage) and Tim Lingard. The "Crusaders" were mostly inspired by Basil Coxon.

1973 Louth Male Voice Choir was re-formed in 1973 (they were photographed here on 25th May 1992) and have sung in many venues. They have given hours of enjoyment to those lucky enough to hear them sing but they struck up a relationship with the Dutch choir, "Albatross", of Newi Pekela, Holland, in 1979 and since then the two choirs have visited each other on an irregular basis.

1966 This was Mr Oxley's class of Kidgate School on an outing to RAF Binbrook to inspect the latest in aircraft technology.

1967 Still going strong: Louth Cricket Club as they chased the Carlton Cup comprised (back row, left to right): J. Hurton, K. Willson, C. Brooks, S. Grant, S. Wootton and L. Lowry. Front row: J. Fearn, A. Dickinson, M. Lee and M. Burton.

1973 Here we see some members of "Albatross" singing in St James' Church. It was intended that each choir visit the other every two years but this has not been the case. Nevertheless they still visit each other and will continue the relationship well into the new millennium. GET

1974 In the reorganisation of local government Percy Fell was the new Mayor of Louth after the dissolution of the old Borough, seen here a few years earlier (in 1966) at a St Michael's Garden Fete. Looking on are (l to r): Sidney ("Sid") Brown, Mrs Fell, Rev. Wright, Mrs Wright, Nicola Barton (who won first prize for the most original costume), Mrs Brown, Mr Warne and Percy Fell. Also in this year President Nixon resigns over Watergate.

1974 Shock-waves went through the Conservative party when Jeffrey Archer (now a best-selling author, art collector and possible Mayor of London) resigned his seat following financial difficulties. He had been MP for Louth since the death of Sir Cyril Osborne in 1969. But that was not the last that Ludensians were to see of Jeffrey Archer - he returned! Seen here in the company of Barbara Dewar, the late Phyllis West and Joan Peart.

1977 In 1977 Arthur Miles (seen here, standing second from right) opened the new cricket pavilion at the London Road Sports Ground. Seen here at an earlier Cricket Club dinner held in the Town Hall (circa 1955), from left to right, are: Alf Cooke, McVicar (who played for Warwickshire), Arthur Miles and Les Coult. Front row, seated: Miss Cooke, Mrs Cooke, Miss Cooke, Mrs Clare Miles and Mrs Ella Coult. BR

1977 The Centenary (or Wesleyan) Chapel in Little Eastgate lost its wonderful interior which was modernised into the stark characterless interior it is today.

1977 Many people in Louth have supported "Jumbulance", the charity which gives elderly or infirm people a holiday break. The late Phyllis West was a great supporter of this charity. Here we see their holiday coach photographed in 1977 with the Mayor of Louth, Gladys Wilcox, in the foreground.   KA

1978 At a charity event in aid of St John's Ambulance, held at Miss Diana Dixon's home, off St Mary's Lane, the Mayor, George Cuppleditch, Mr Kirkham and Bishop Colin (Bishop of Grimsby) were present. Bishop Colin was an excellent after-dinner speaker and something of a raconteur.

1978 On 15th August Tony Espin was photographed on the steps of Louth Town Hall following his Channel swim (it took him 14hrs and 13mins to swim from England to France). He is being congratulated by the Mayor, whilst many familiar faces look on, including Gordon Webb (past Editor of the Louth Standard), the late Percy Fell, Ken Dewar and the Town Clerk, Leslie ("Jock") Riddick. KA

Louth has produced its share of centenarians. Mrs Smalley (seen here) reached her 100th birthday and continued to shop in the Cornmarket!

1979 Monks Dyke enjoyed its Jubilee on 2nd April. Amongst the group of familiar names, sadly there are many who are not amongst us any more, including Dr and Mrs Redfern (front row, extreme right), and next to them Roosevelt Wilkinson (Mayor of Louth in 1964 and 1971). Ted Smith (back row, extreme right, with glasses and white moustache). Also recognisable are Martin Stocks, Harry Younger and Ted Savage. In May of this year Margaret Thatcher became Britain's first woman Prime Minister.   KA

1980 In October John Bourne died, aged 71. John Kendall Bourne, a local historian, was the grandson of John Bourne of Dalby Hall, who married Mary Tennyson (Alfred Lord Tennyson's aunt). He lived in the Manor House, Eastgate, and was something of a magpie, hoarding all sorts of things throughout his life. One of his claims was to possess a set of keys which unlocked doors through a network of tunnels from St James' Church to Louth Park Abbey.

1980 Buster Mottram, the tennis star, came to Louth to encourage youngsters. He was seen here outside the newly erected Sports Hall with Mayor George Arliss. George Arliss (no relation to the star of the same name) worked for most of his life in Hong Kong, was captured by the Japanese and was interned as a POW. He returned to Louth on his retirement. From left to right are Jim Walmsley, Noel Clark, Mike Lugg (the tennis umpire), Buster Mottram, John Needham (Mayor of Louth in 1981), George Arliss, Jack Robertson, Sandra Everitt and Pete Smith. KA

1982 David Smith left the Wheatsheaf pub in Westgate. He had been the tenant since 1973 when he took over from Cyril Graves. He is seen here offering a stirrup cup of ale to the Bishop of Lincoln Simon Phipps circa 1976.

1982 Mention horses and I automatically think of the Southwold Hunt, which has met many times in Louth. This photograph was taken at the beginning of the season, outside the Bluebell Inn at Belchford, and it is a young Ann Laverack on the horse.

1983 John Sellick (Alliance Party) gave Peter Tapsell (Conservative) a fright in the General Election. Seen here in the 1987 local election, he is in the centre of picture. With him are, left to right: Rob Cook, Dorothy Grant (who became Mayor of Louth in 1991), John Sellick, David Bolland and Mike Birmingham. GET

There have been many claims to the title of the authority on Louth history. But I can confess that Harry Smith, who was 86 years old in 1983, was certainly one of them. Born at 7 Upgate, the son of a tinsmith, he served with the 5th Battalion of the Lincolnshire Regiment. After the war he worked at Eve & Ranshaw, then with Harrison's (the builders) until his retirement, when he worked part-time for Bexon's. When he died he left over 2,500 slides of Lincolnshire, mostly of Louth.

1983 Miss Kent died of pneumonia in January at Crowtree Lane Hospital, aged 90. She was born in Lincoln and taught in numerous households with royal connections, including Spain, Italy, Germany and Austria, before teaching at Brampton College, Eastfield Road. She will be remembered as quite a character in Louth, especially for her dislike of motorised traffic! This portrait of her was painted by Elaine Drewery of Tiggywinkles Hedgehog Hospital, Authorpe. Elaine's daughter, Corinne Drewery, sang in the pop group "Swing Out Sister". GET

1983 On 24th April the Rector of Louth, the Rev. David Owen, welcomed his predecessor at Louth, the Archdeacon of Lincoln, the Venerable Michael Adie, who was to become Bishop of Guildford on 30th June of this year.

1984 At the Conservative Association's dinner on 1st December, in South Elkington, Sir Peter and Lady Tapsell were present. From left to right they are Mr and Mrs John Myers, Sir Peter and Lady Gabrielle Tapsell, the late Mrs Cathy Stubbs and Joe Wallis (the farmer from Biscathorpe). Sir Peter Tapsell has been a Member of Parliament for a Lincolnshire constituency since 1966 and before that for West Nottingham (1959-1964) and at one time was personal assistant to Sir Anthony Eden. He was knighted in 1985.

1983 At the Louth Crib Service, Father Travis of St Michael's presided. With him are the Mayor, Frank Michael, Town Clerk Fred Weir and Councillor Peter Conway. GET

1984 The Rev. David Owen presiding over a Teddy Bears' Service in St James'. GET

1984 To try something different Mayor Stan Ward took a bath into the Market Place to raise money for charity. It was a daring and new innovation, but it worked!

1984 As an incentive to learn road safety procedures and enact them, a competition was held. The winners were awarded a free ticket to see "Pinocchio" at the Playhouse. These were the lucky winners with Inspector Trevor Grant, Ralph Dalton (Manager of the Playhouse) and PC Keith Sharpe.   GET

Seth Armstrong, of the TV soap "Emmerdale", visited Louth to promote Westwood Lawnmowers. Seen here, Seth (whose real name is Stan Richards) mixed charm with commercialism and won over many fans including Alan Bexon.   GET

1984 Louth Playgoers presented "A Christmas Carol", with Philip Skipworth as Bob Cratchit (a role which David Collings, who lived at Upgate, played in the Albert Finney film version of "Scrooge").   GET

1985 The news-vendor George Standley was photographed on 17th October. He delivered newspapers throughout his life, including to the hospital, and was a well-known Louth character.

1986 1st October saw the opening of the Festival of Flowers in St James' Church, coinciding with the 430th anniversary of the Lincolnshire Rising of 1536. From 1st-5th October, there was a series of talks including one given on Miss Wintringham, MP for Louth and the first English woman to sit in Parliament. Nancy Astor might lay claim to have been the first woman in the House of Commons but she was American by birth. Miss Wintringham, of Little Grimsby Hall, who took her seat as the Liberal MP for Louth in the twenties after the death of her husband, was the first English woman.

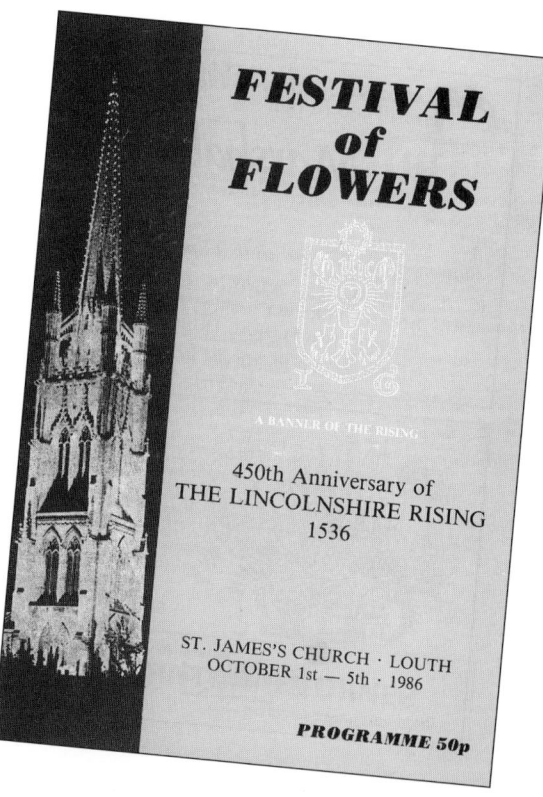

1987 This was a Louth Playgoers' production of "Pygmalion", by George Bernard Shaw, which ran from 9th-14th November. The familiar face of Ken Watkinson is dressed in top-hat and sporting a moustache. GET

On 21st May the Duchess of Gloucester opened "Smilies" Clubhouse, off St Bernards Avenue. The last time a Gloucester had visited Louth was during the Second World War when the old Duke of Gloucester was photographed outside Lacey Gardens. GET

1987 The Louth Lions' Charter Dinner. The Louth Lions have given to various needy charities over the years and continue to carry out good works, usually without recognition. Lions President Peter Oatway is pictured third from left. GET

1987 Mayor Roy Gathercole and civic party post outside the Town Hall for a group photograph. Sadly, many of them have since passed away - such as Councillors Jack Winn, Stan Ward and Joyce Munslow. On the right of this photo is the Mayor's Officer Mr Chris Cooper. GET

1987 On 11th October the snooker champion, Joe Johnson, visited Louth to hand over £1,000 to the Carl Stocks Trust Fund, which was formed after Carl was in a car accident which left him paralysed. Seen here in the centre of the photo is Charles Baron.

1988 HRH Princess Anne (now Princess Royal) arrived in Louth to open the Livestock Centre at Louth Cattle Market. Seen here, she was greeted by the Mayor, John Richard Macdonald, and proceeded to officially open the Centre. Princess Anne was to return ten years later, in 1998, to visit "Sense" in Old Mill Park.

1989 And a young Mike Kinnaird, presenter with Radio Lincolnshire, is accepting a cheque on behalf of the radio station. If anyone were to tot up the amount of money that Louth has handed over to charity in the post-war period it would be staggering. GET

1989 Hannah Hauxwell, author of "Daughter of the Dales" and personality of Yorkshire TV, paid a few visits to Louth in the '80s. She felt quite at home in Louth which in many respects resembles her native Yorkshire. She was pictured here with Mr Marshall of the flower shop in the Cornmarket.

1990 There have been very few private schools in Louth in the twentieth century. Miss Surfleet's in Gospelgate (now the home of Dr and Mrs Oke), Fir Close (now a nursing home), Brampton College (featured on page 57) and Greenwich House. In September Greenwich House School moved into its premises on High Holme Road. Prior to this, Mr and Mrs Brindle had run a creche from their private residence, also called Greenwich House, off Crowtree Lane. Here we see some of the pupils and staff winning an award in 1992. They are, from left to right, Mrs MacGregor (now Mrs Brewer) and Mrs J. Brindle with pupils Sarah Vamplew, Lizzie Ellis, Edward Brindle.   GET

In October Ian Botham's charity walk for Leukaemia Research came through Louth. Seen here walking down Mercer Row in the company of the Mayor, Joyce Munslow, Botham has walked 3,500 miles to raise more than £3 million for the Leukemia Research Fund.   GET

1990 On 25th August those two popular Coronation Street residents, "Mavis and Derek Wilton" (actors Thelma Barlow and Peter Baldwin), opened the Manby Show. GET

The display of traction engines was awesome! A bit like a regimental march past. GET

1991 Here we see Macdonald's traction engine, which is only brought out on special occasions, photographed on 4th November. GET

1991 The ladies of Louth Golf Club; they are from left to right Jean Fenner, Marguerite Miles, a lady in a cap, Jo Parrish, the late Sue Randell, Marjorie Watkinson, Margaret Craven, Val Laughton, Elsie Farrow, Ann King, Joyce Templeton, Shirley Strickland, Cath Hammond and Joy Chambers. GET

1991 On 13th March the familiar face of strongman Geoff Capes was in Louth (seen here with budgerigar). Although known as a strongman and possibly even as a policeman – he is also a budgerigar breeder and judge.　　　　　　　　　　　　　　　　　　　　　　　　　　GET

1991 On 30th June Louth's long-awaited bypass was officially opened. There had been proposals for a bypass before the Second World War but it took some time before these were implemented. Among the various floats and assortment of vehicles that crawled along the bypass that day was a selection of tractors.　　　　　　　　　　　　　　　　　　　　　　　　　　GET

1992 A visit from the famous rugby winger, Rory Underwood, encouraged youngsters to appreciate the game. From left to right (back row) they were: John Williams (coach), G. Willows, M. Pearce, B. Ranshaw, D. Brown, J. Myers, A. Pendegrass, B. John. Front row: J. Harvey, B. Williams, Rory Underwood, M. Keeler (captain) and J. Bunce.

1992 No doubt inspired by Rory Underwood's visit, this group of rugby hopefuls was photographed at Cordeaux High School on 26th October. Mr P. McLeod is the P.E. teacher on the left.

1992 When Kenneth Clarke MP visited Louth, he was a rising star in the Conservative Party and is seen here talking to Mrs Jackson, Mrs Baron and the late Miss Diana Dixon. Peter Craig, of the Grimsby Evening Telegraph, is visible in the background. GET

As part of the Louth Festival in 1992, the deaf percussionist Evelyn Glennie gave a memorable performance in St James' (seen here on 27th May with three helpers). GET

1992 On 6th October local singing star now-turned actress, Barbara Dickson, declared the "Sense" house open and met some of its young residents. The committee (who formed in 1989) had raised a total of £120,000 to build the house and set it off running. Nearly one third of this total came from the Lions. GET

1992 On 22nd September Phil Brown, the Olympic athlete, paid a visit to Louth. He is seen here with a group of Cordeaux High School students. Liz Finlayson, the Louth Leader photographer, walking in the background.

1992 That popular event, the annual pantomime. This was some of the cast of Peter Pan seen at rehearsals on 9th November, 1992.   GET

1993 Lincolnshire Road Car celebrated 65 years of service in Louth and well deserved too!   GET

1993 There was a procession of St John's Ambulance on 20th October to attend a service in St James'. In the procession are the familiar faces of Jeremy Blower and Cecil Jollands, whose forebear was a previous Rector of St James'.   GET

1993 Photographed outside the Beaumont Hotel, Victoria Road, was the late broadcaster Brian Redhead, shaking hands with Dan Carron at a fund-raising event in aid of the MRI Scanner Appeal, Grimsby.
GET

1993 The 1990's saw the emergence of a large number of charity shops in Louth. This was the British Heart Foundation shop on the site of the old Ship & Horns pub. Note: Meridian House had not been built at this time.
GET

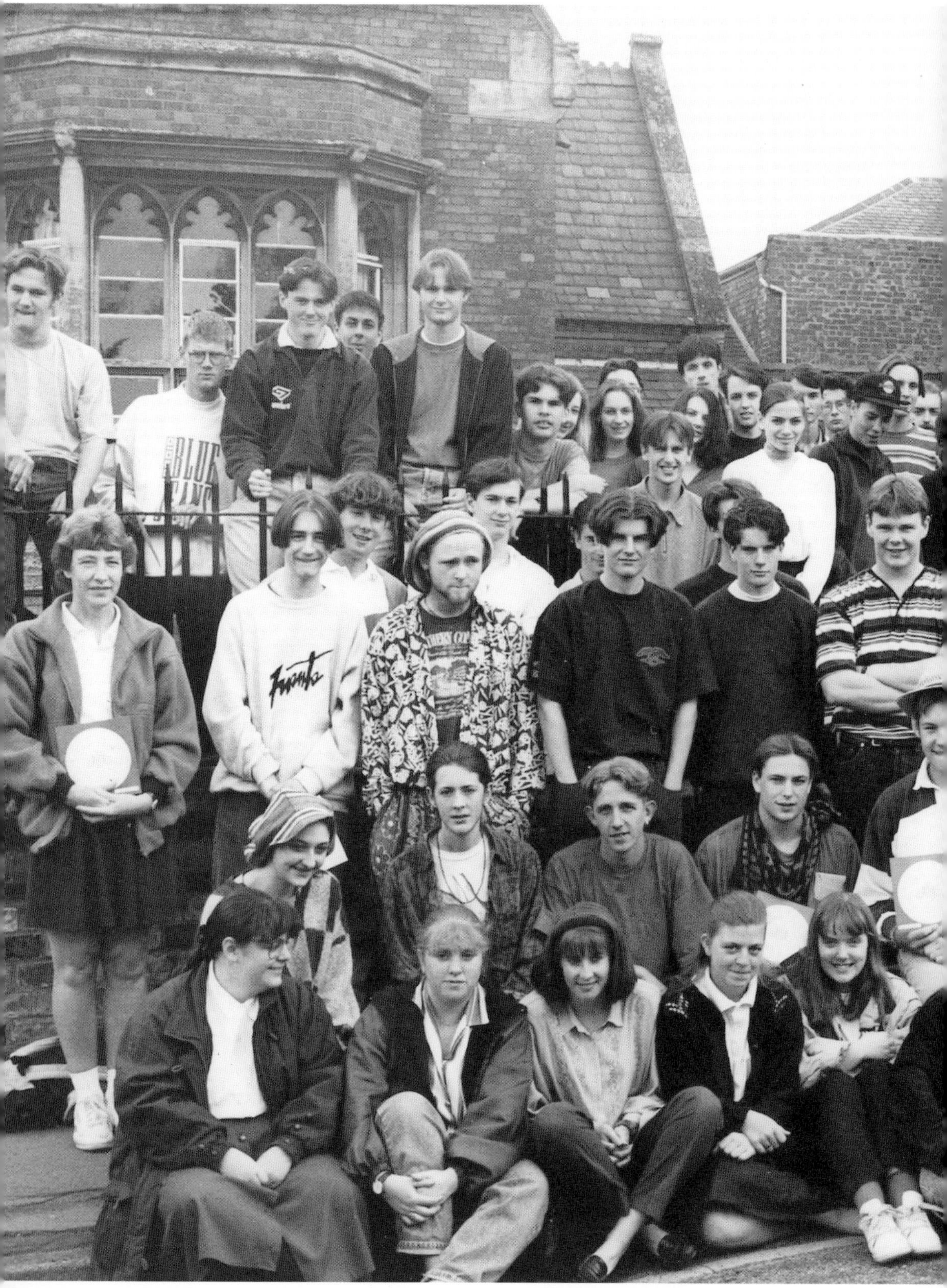

On 26th June pupils of King Edward VI were photographed in School House Lane. The familiar face of Janet West is on the left and Avtar Bath on the right. GET

108   LOUTH The Twentieth Century

1993 The popular headmaster of Kidgate School, Stuart Sizer, acting as a D.J. at the Louth Christmas Market.

1994 The Grimsby Evening Telegraph organised a "Rock Open" at "My Father's Moustache" (opposite the front entrance to Cordeaux High School). Here we see Graham Fellows (formerly "Jilted John") and Tim Greenfield of the Evening Telegraph, who has since left the Telegraph and now works for the "Royal Gazette" in the Bahamas.   GET

1994 "Remember, remember the fifth of November" - and these two have with their barrel of gunpowder.   GET

1995 The first manufacturing factory on the newly formed Industrial Estate was Davenport Stannard, setting up in May 1969 (originally they worked out of the wooden hut on the site of the Victoria Road Swimming Pool). In 1995 they raised £800 to give to two charities, St. Bernard's School and "Sense" (each receiving £400 each). Seen here are from left to right: Mike Warren, Sarah Coppin, Annette Hall, a "Sense" representative, Jeff Grewcock (M.D.), another "Sense" representative and Helen Rice-Mundy. This year the controversial novelist and campaigner for author's rights, Bridgid Brophy (1929-1995) died in Fir Close Nursing Home.

1996 Princess Alexandra came to Louth to officially open the wards at the back of Louth Hospital, even though they had been in use for some time. Seen here talking to Mayor Gus Robertson and sharing a private joke, she carried out her duties with dignity. Sadly the tree which she planted on this occasion was vandalised. GET

1996 Although the Cattle Market is much diminished in size and turnover from those halcyon days in the forties and fifties when it was at its peak, it still operates. In this photograph it is Billy Hunter holding the small calf, whilst James Laverack, of John Taylors, is the auctioneer.

1997 Eileen Ballard (the Mayor) was photographed on 11th June, flanked by (on the left) Sgt Knaggs and (right) Inspector Rod Bell - assisting them with their enquiries perhaps?!   GET

1997 Saw the untimely death of Marcus Brown (1960-1997), whose funeral service was held in St James' on 6th March. Marcus, nicknamed "the gentle giant", managed the Peugeot dealership on Newbridge Hill. He is seen here on the right of the photo promoting a go-cart event for youngsters.   GET

1998 David Kaye, Mayor of Louth, standing at the back of this group with white beard has written "Discovering Lincolnshire" for Shire publications, "Fowler of Louth" (the life of James Fowler architect) and many articles for "Lincolnshire Life". He is sending out his Christmas greetings from the Louth Rotary Club float on 8th December.   GET

1999 Professor Philip Norton was created Lord Norton of Louth in Tony Blair's Honours List. Seen here handing out prizes in St James' Church to Grammar School pupils on 23 December 1991, when John Haden was Headmaster (1982-1991). The new Lord Norton, who himself was educated at Lacey Gardens and King Edward VI, saw the honour as overwhelming.
GET

LIST OF LOUTH MAYORS

1900 Hurd Hickling	1933 Ernest Harry Thompson	1967 Reginald M. Cross
1901 Mark Smith	1934 Albert Ernest Maxey	1968 Gladys P. Wilcox
1902 Mark Smith	1935 Albert Ernest Maxey	1969 Ronald H. Brackenbury
1903 Frederick M. Thompson	1936 John Richard Coney	1970 Robin Brumby
1904 Henry David Simpson	1937 Albert Herbert Wright	1971 Roosevelt Wilkinson
1905 Mark Smith	1938 Laurance John Lill	1972 Charles O. Everitt
1906 Richard Dawson	1939 Laurance John Lill	1973 Frank Macdonald
1907 Hurd Hickling	1940 Ernest Harry Thompson	1974 Percy Fell
1908 Herbert Sharpley	1941 Albert Ernest Maxey	1975 Peter Graham Smith
1909 Thomas Gelsthorp	1942 Evan William Macdonald	1976 Alfred Stanley Ward
1910 George Blaze	1943 George Harold Taylor	1977 Gladys Pacey Wilcox
1911 Thomas Gelsthorp	1944 John Robert Sanderson	1978 George A. Cuppleditch
1912 Thomas Gelsthorp	1945 William Rowson	1979 Frank Macdonald
1913 Richard Maltby	1946 John Carveley Shelton	1980 George Arliss
1914 HurdHickling	1947 Wilfred Alex Slack	1981 John Robert Needham
1915 Christopher Adlard	1949 Arthur W. Jaines	1982 Kenneth Ronald West
1916 Christopher Adlard	1950 Maurice Hall	1983 George A. Cuppleditch
1917 Richard Dawson	1951 John C. Wherry	1984 Alfred Stanley Ward
1918 Sydney H. Jackson	1952 John H. Starsmore	1985 Frank Raymond Michael
1919 William Lacey	1953 Frank Macdonald	1986 Conny Jardine
1920 William Lacey	1954 William Robert Burr	1987 Roy Gathercole
1921 Henry Stanley Walker	1955 Albert Ernest Maxey	1988 John Richard Macdonald
1922 Henry Stanley Walker	1956 Albert Ernest Maxey	1989 Sandra Jean Ingleton
1923 James Lill	1957 William Patchett	1990 Joyce Mildred Munslow
1924 William S. Sowerby	1958 Ronald H. Brackenbury	1991 Dorothy Grant
1925 Sydney H. Jackson	1959 John H. Starsmore	1992 David Shepherd
1926 Frank Henry Fieldsend	1960 Charles W. Dunham	1993 John Dean
1927 Henry Higson Simpson	1961 W. R. Cecil Simpson	1994 Clive Finch
1928 Percy Parker	1962 Arthur McNeany	1995 Fergus Robertson
1929 Albert Ernest Maxey	1963 Neville J. Nicholson	1996 Margaret Ottoway
1930 Bert Appleby	1964 Roosevelt Wilkinson	1997 Eileen Ballard
1931 John Palmer Becket	1965 A. Elizabeth Hardy	1998 David Kaye
1932 Jesse Rushforth	1966 Percy Fell	1999 David Skinner

ACKNOWLEDGEMENTS

I am particularly grateful to the late Brian Howe, the late James Baildom, Tom Barton, Mick Lee, Ann Laverack, Gus Robertson, David Smith, Peter Craig, Peter Moore (Editor of the Grimsby Evening Telegraph), Linda Roberts, Peter Chapman and, last but not least, Louth Secretarial Services for typing this manuscript so carefully.

Picture Reference

AJ – Arthur James;   LH – "Les" Howe;   BR – Bert Rawlings;   KA – Ken Atterby;
GET – Grimsby Evening Telegraph